MINDFULNESS

Mandalas and Paisley

ADULT COLORING BOOKS

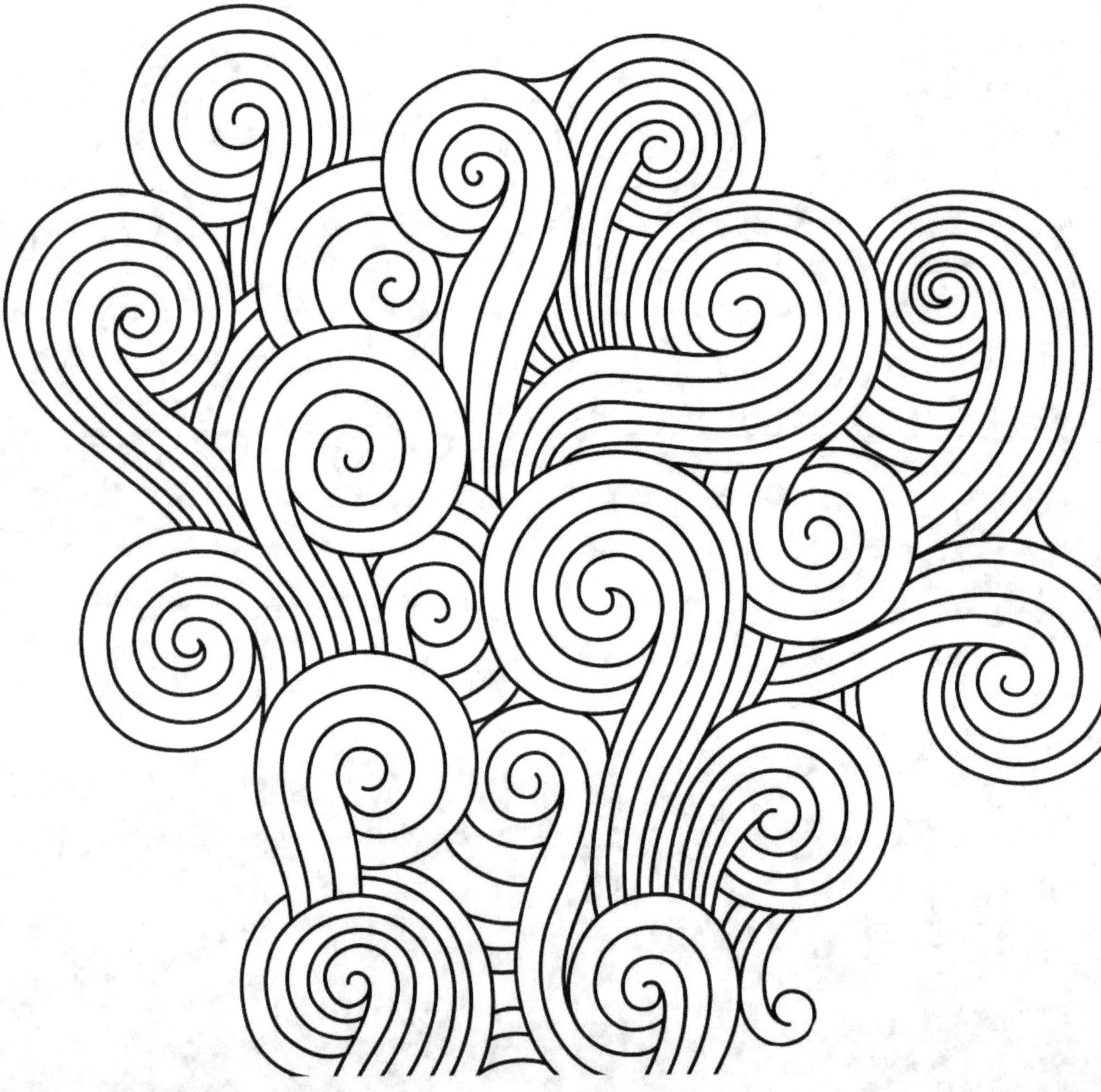

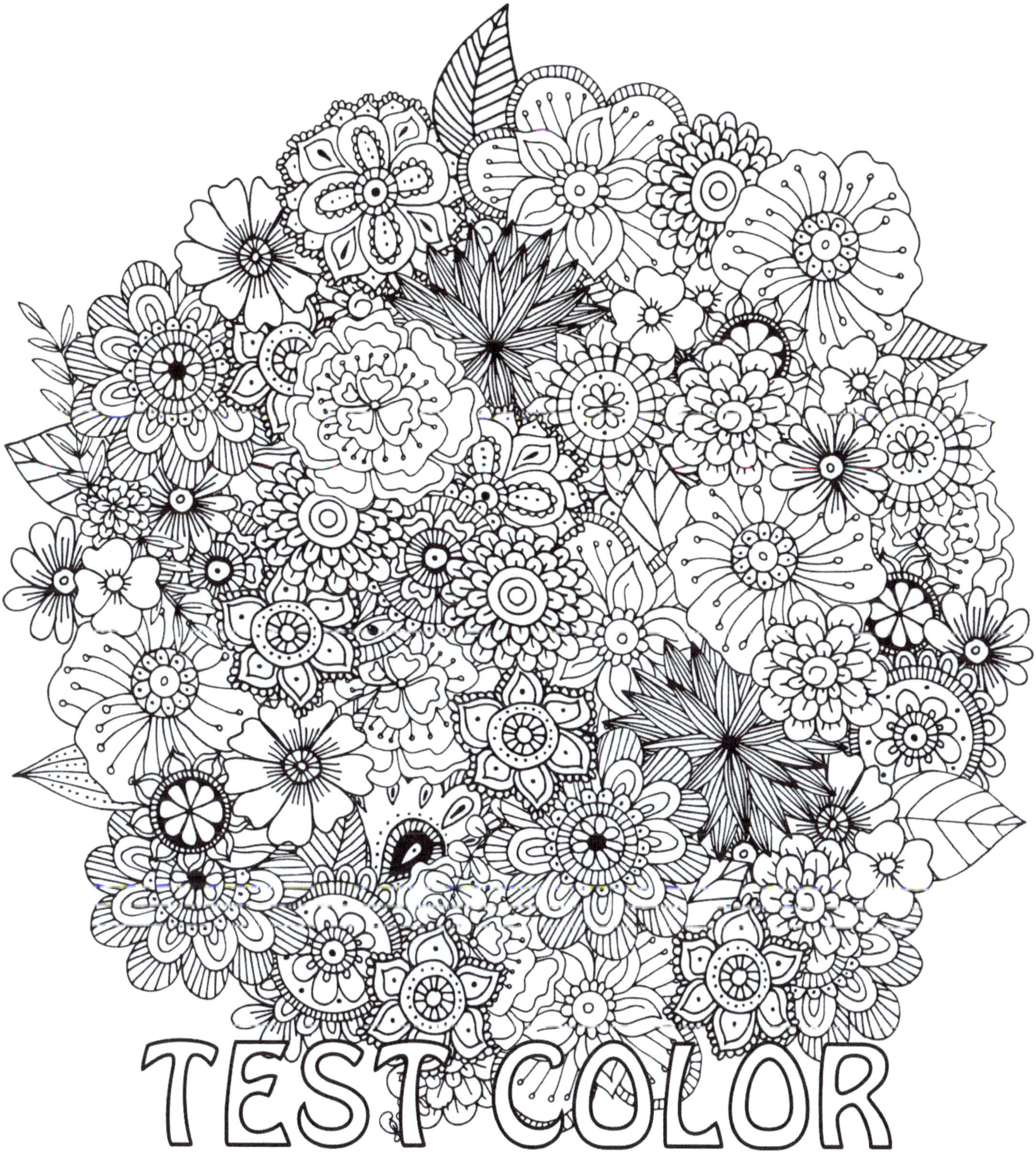

TEST COLOR

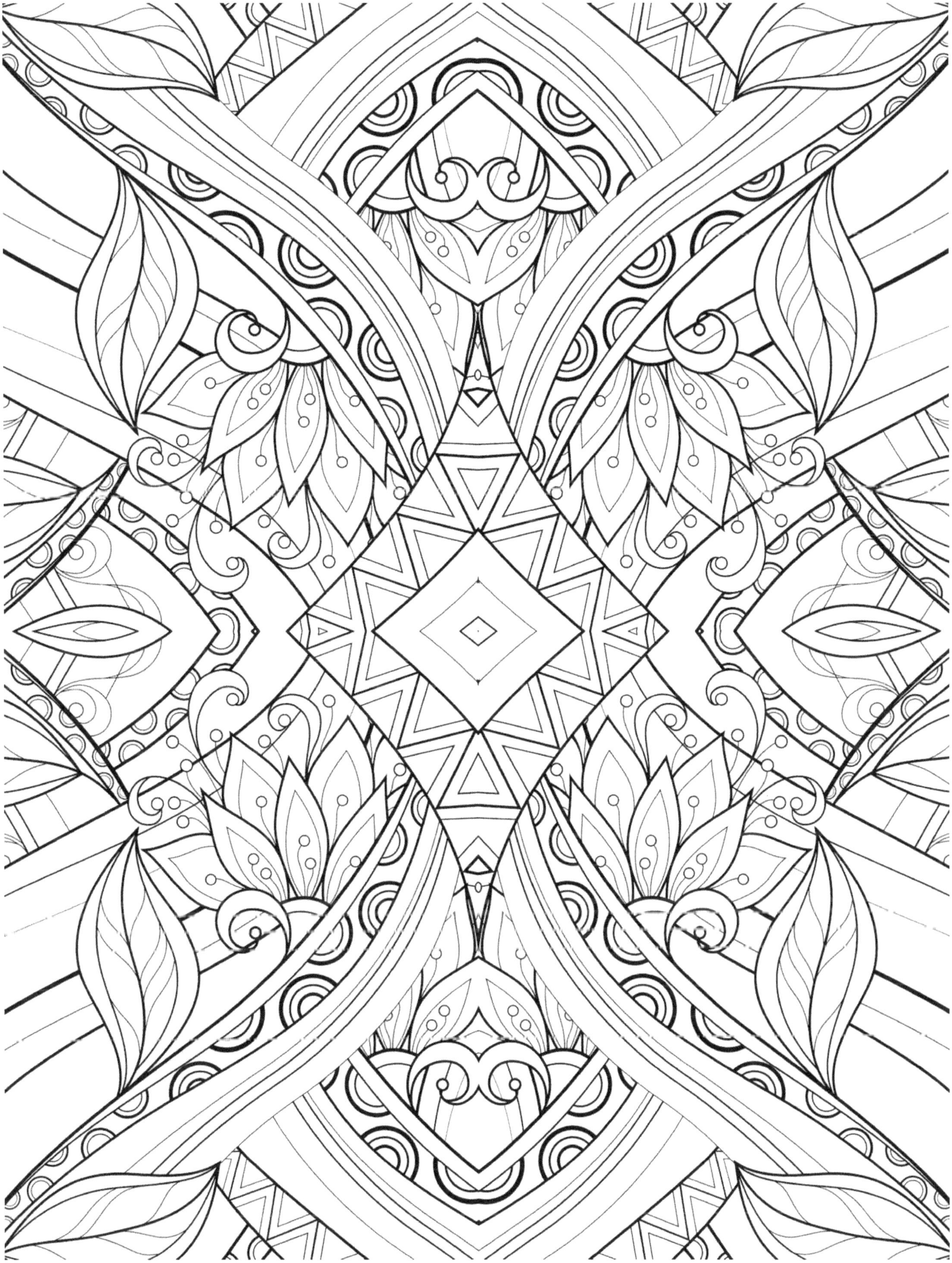

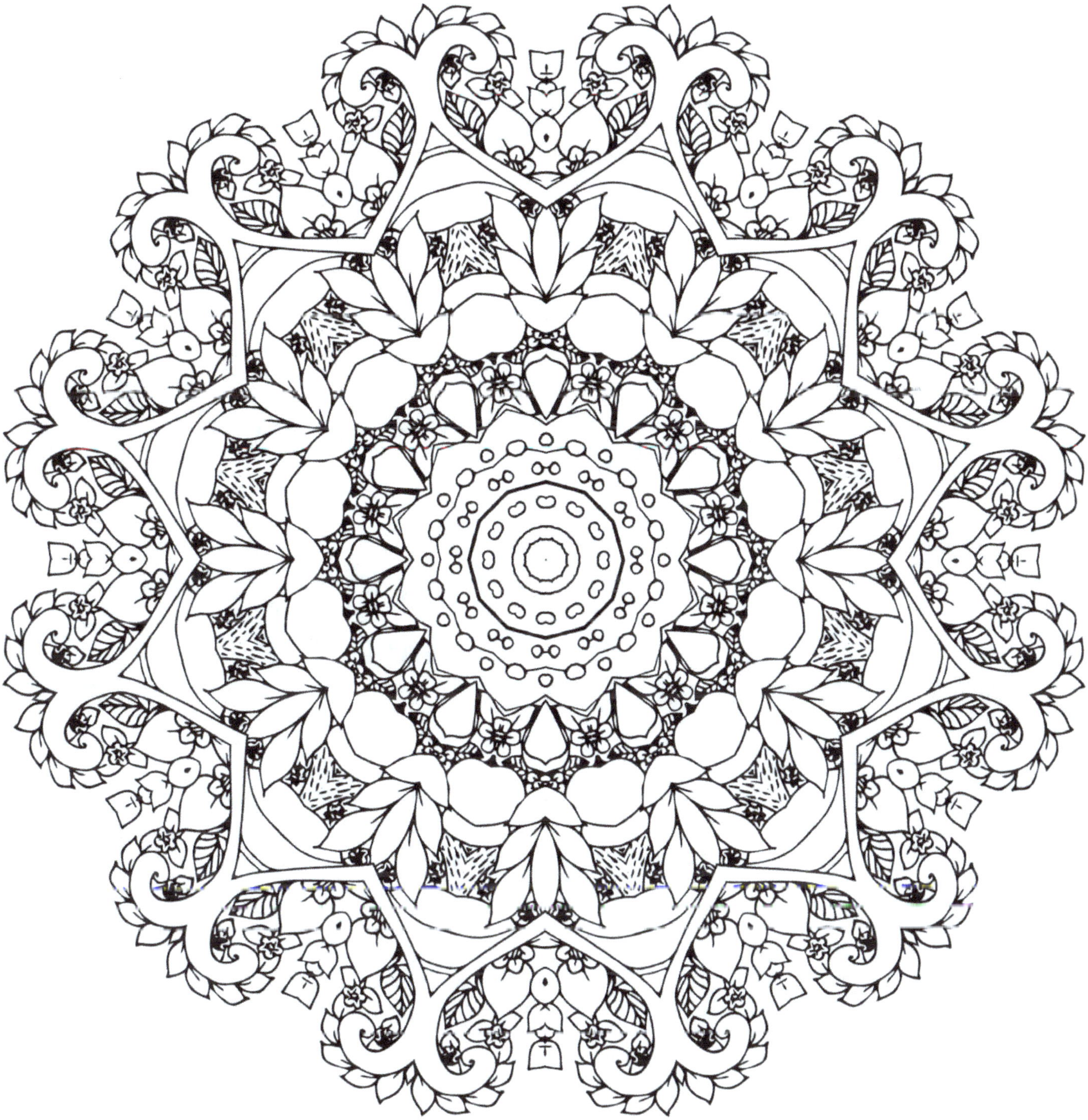

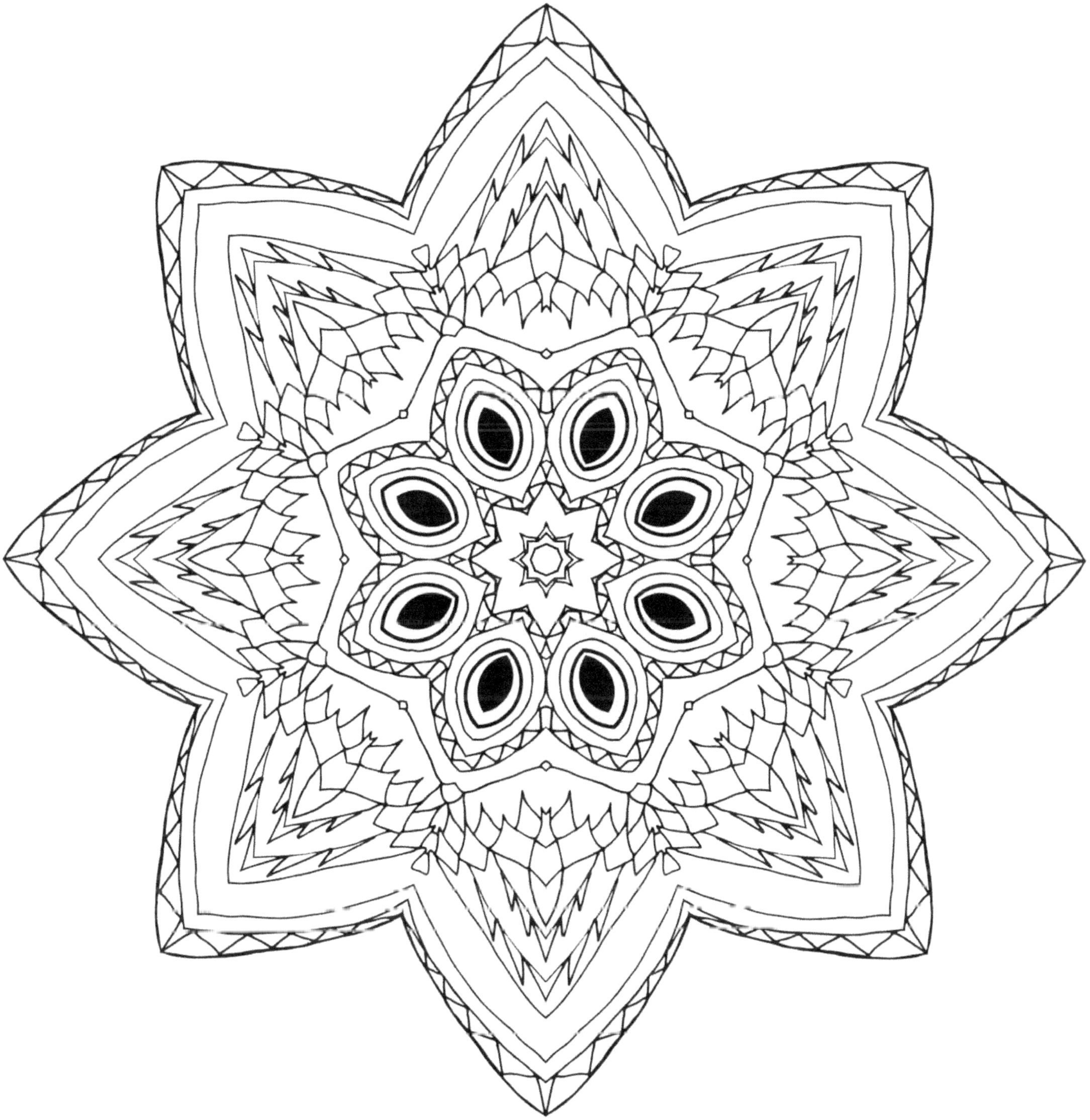

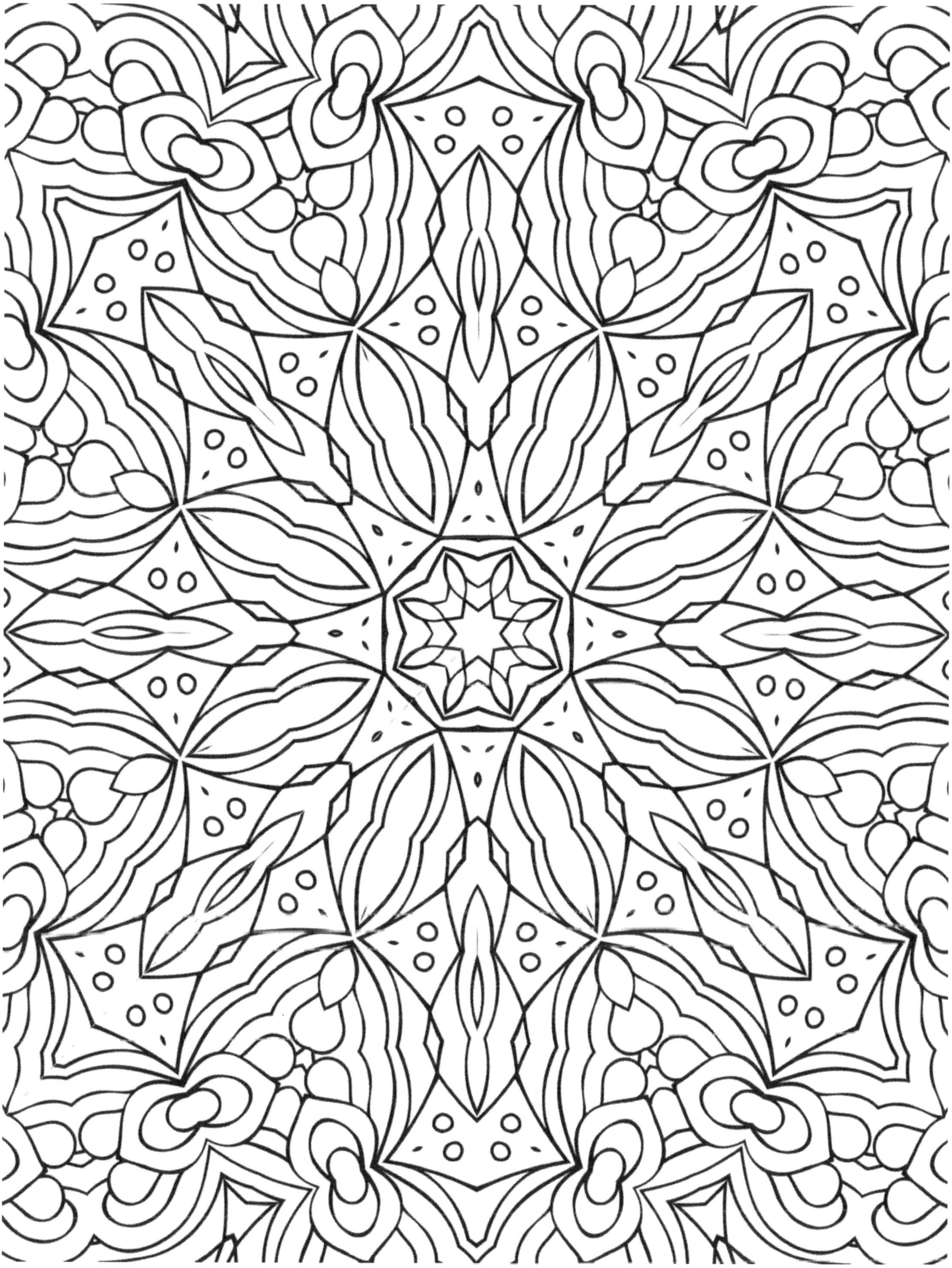

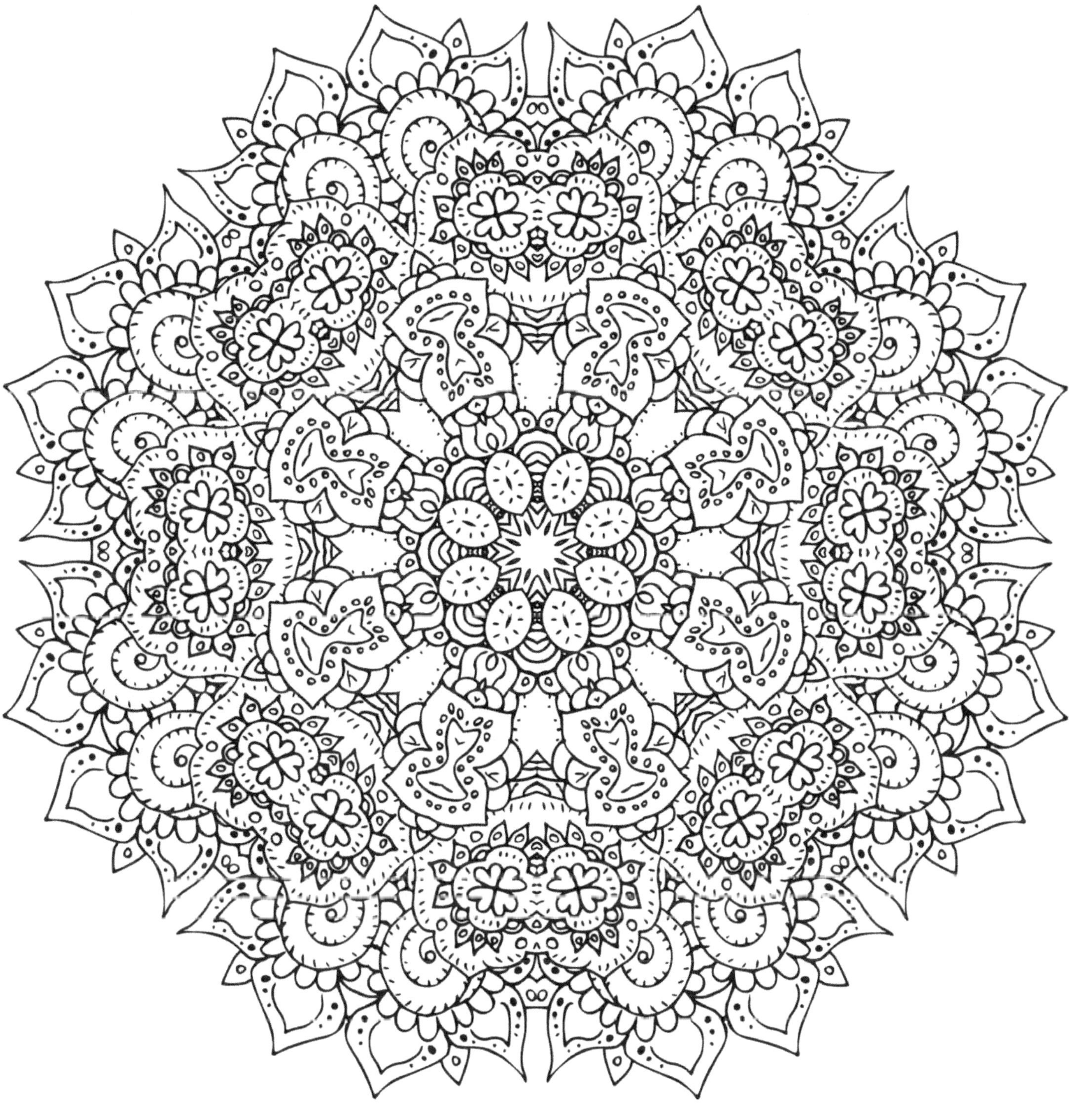

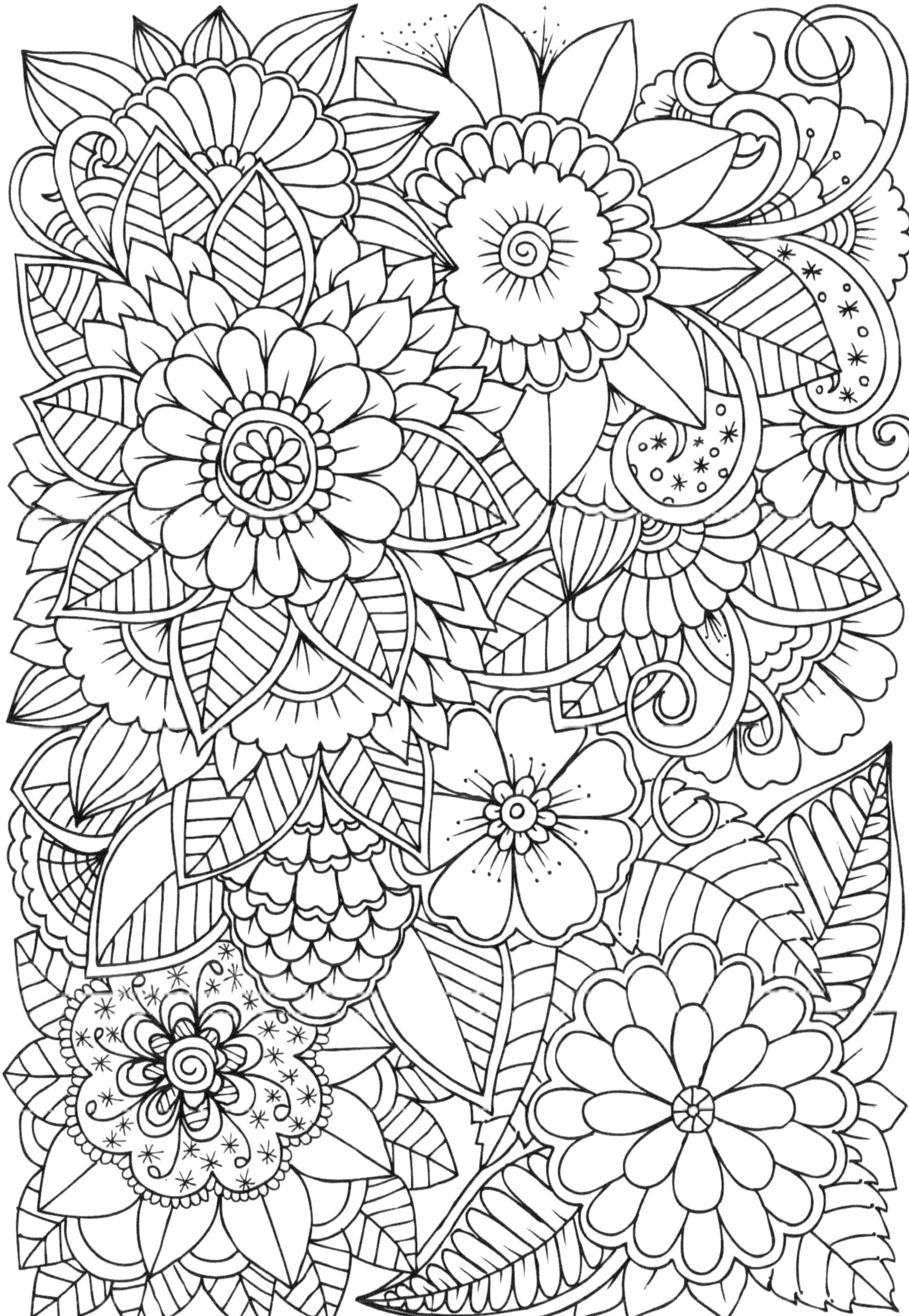

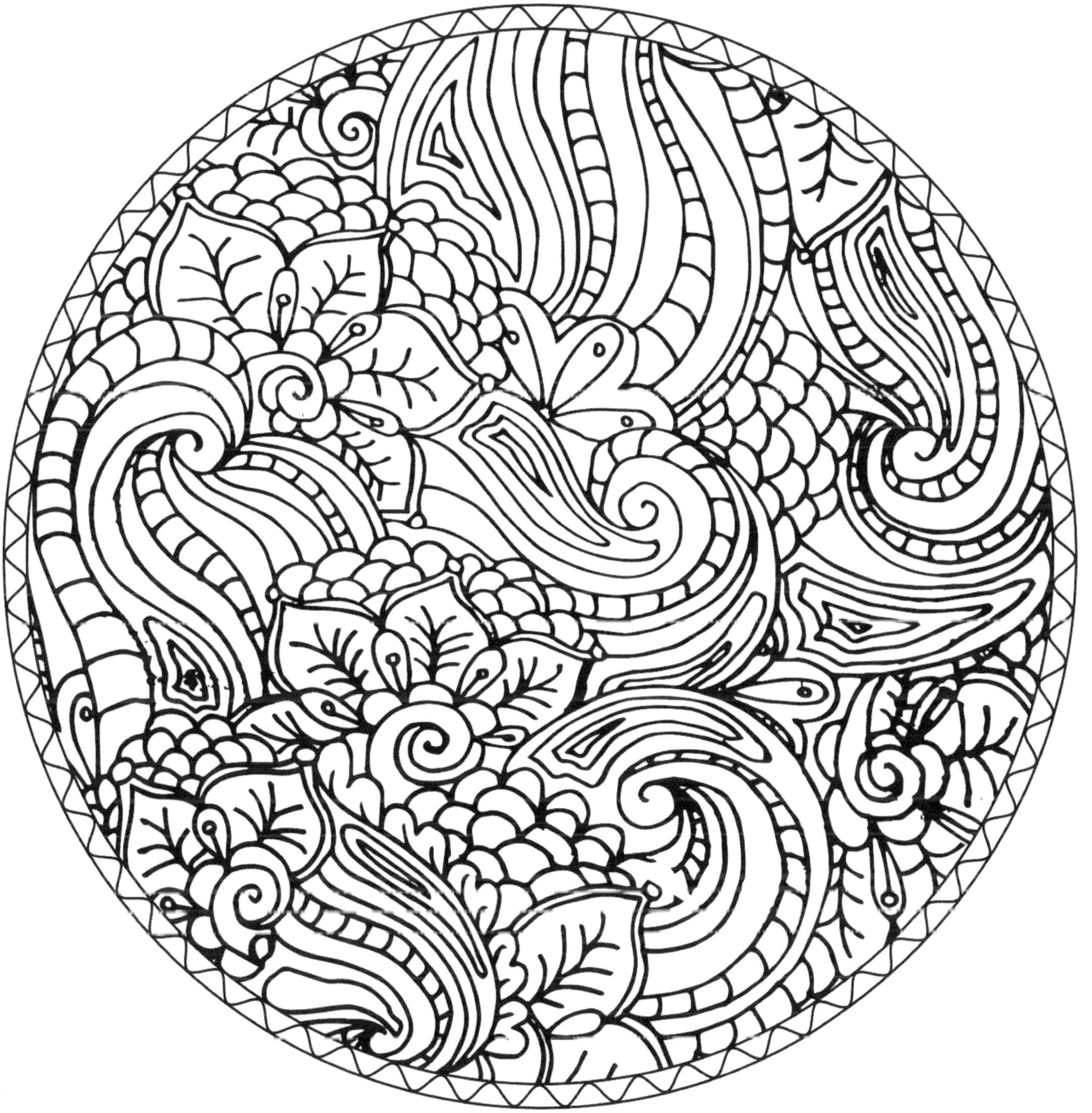

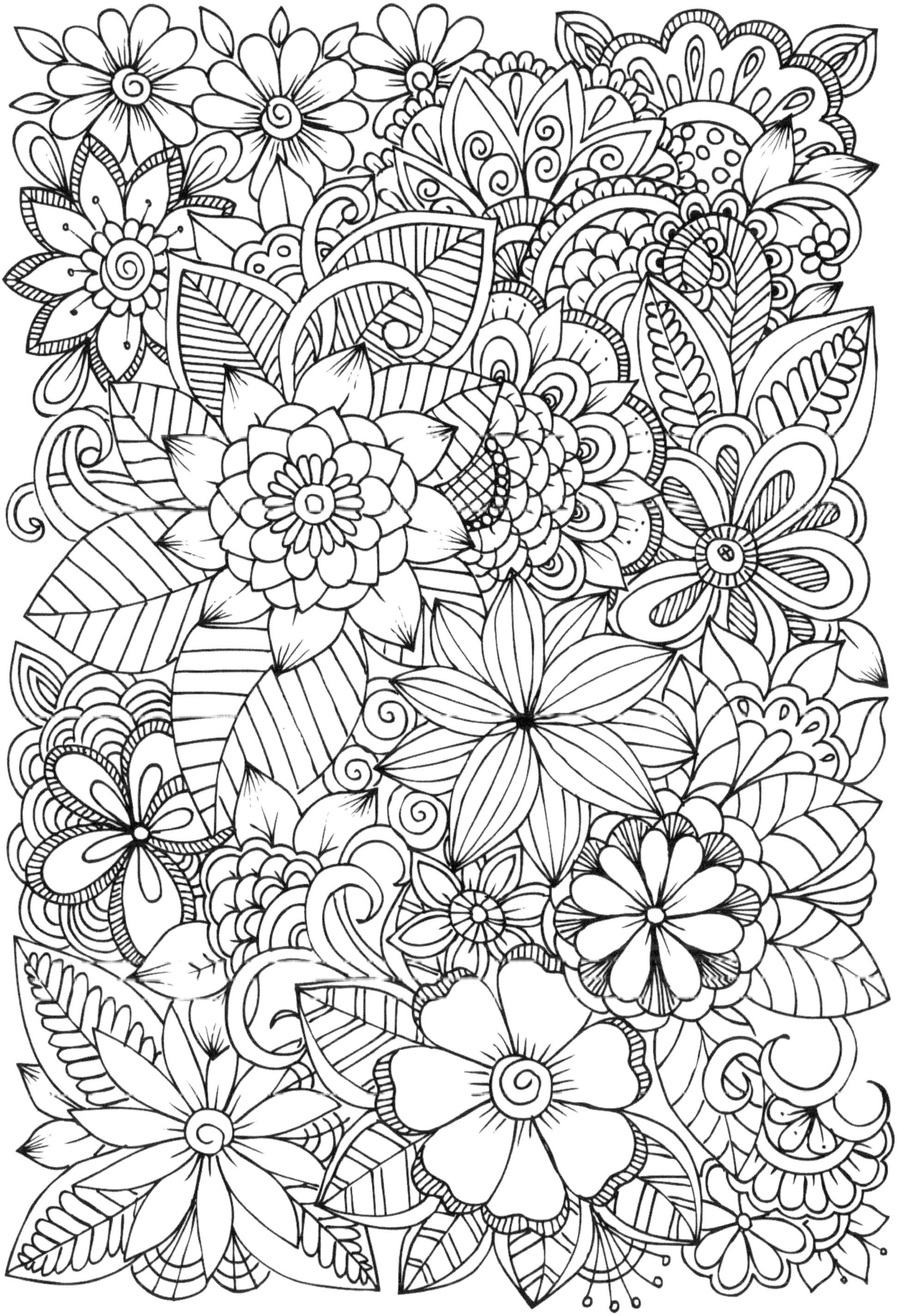

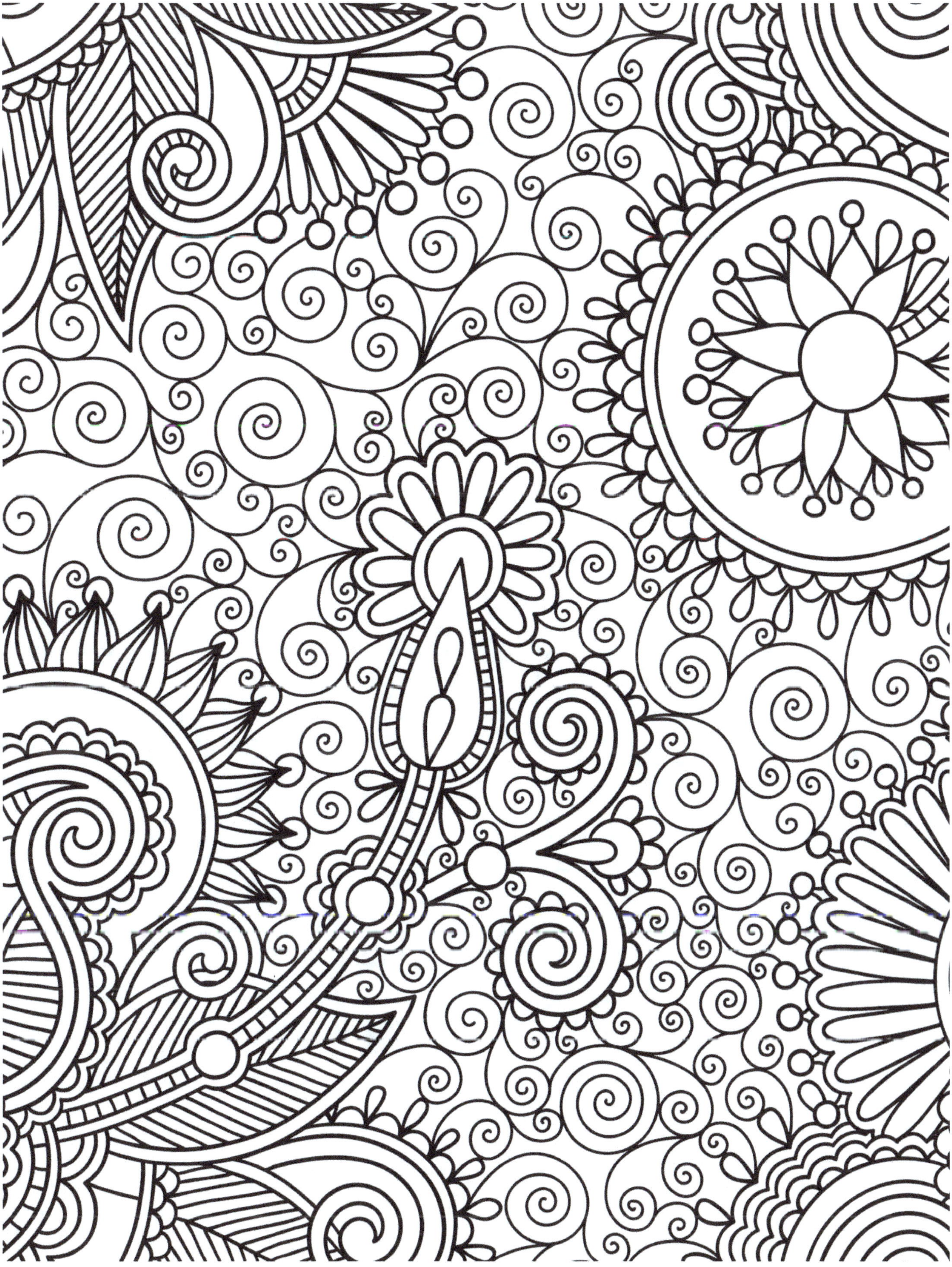

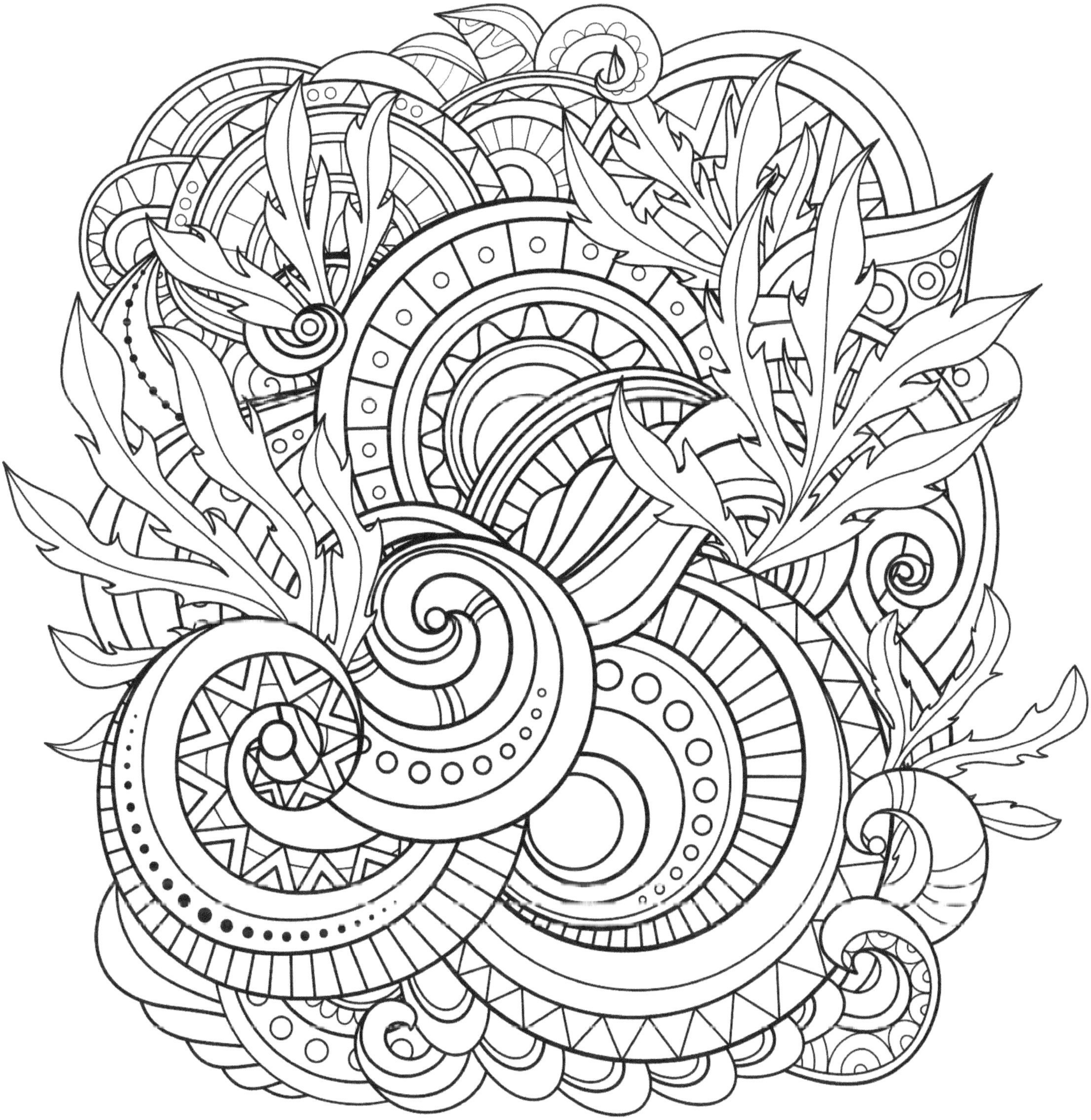

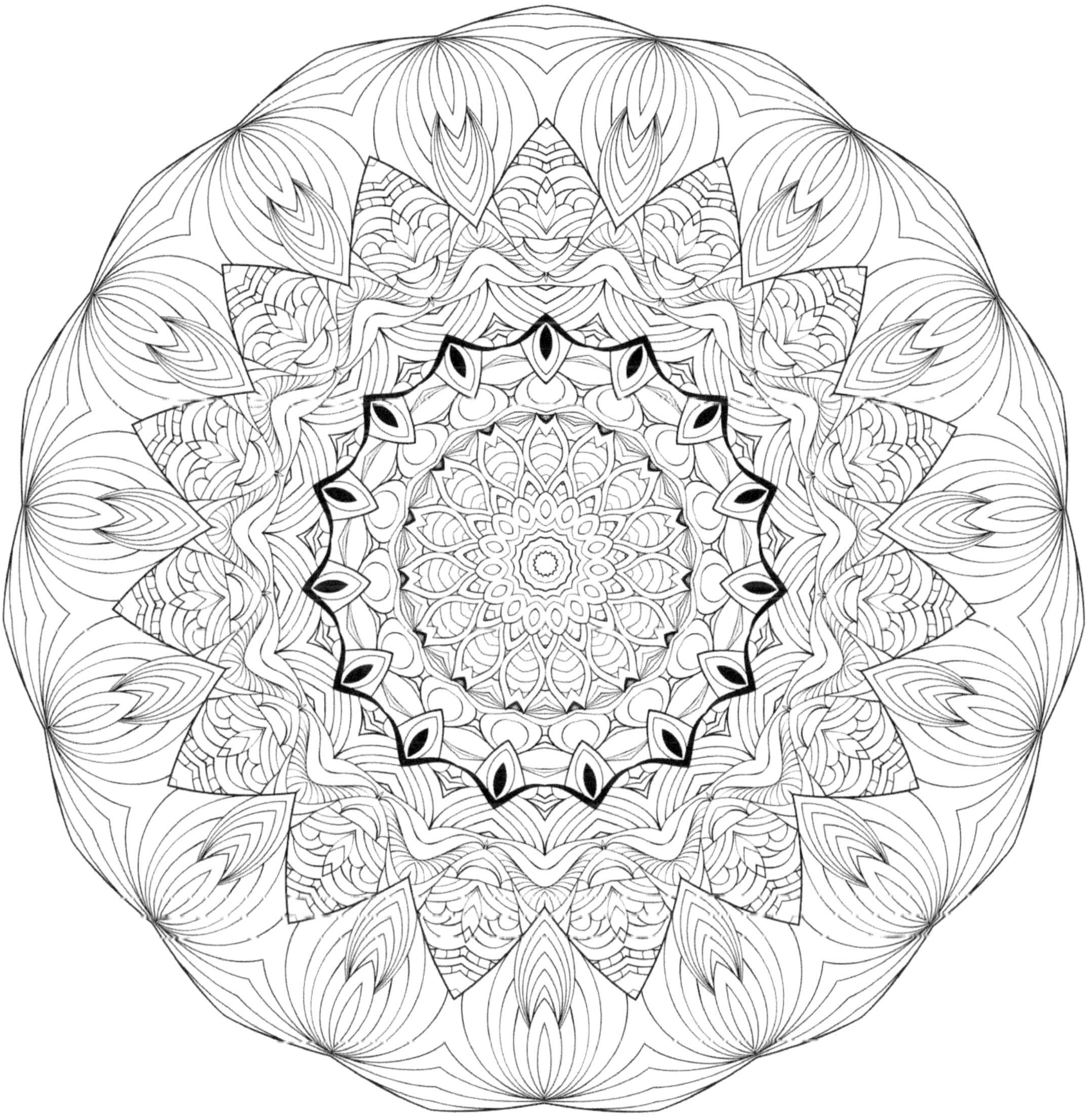

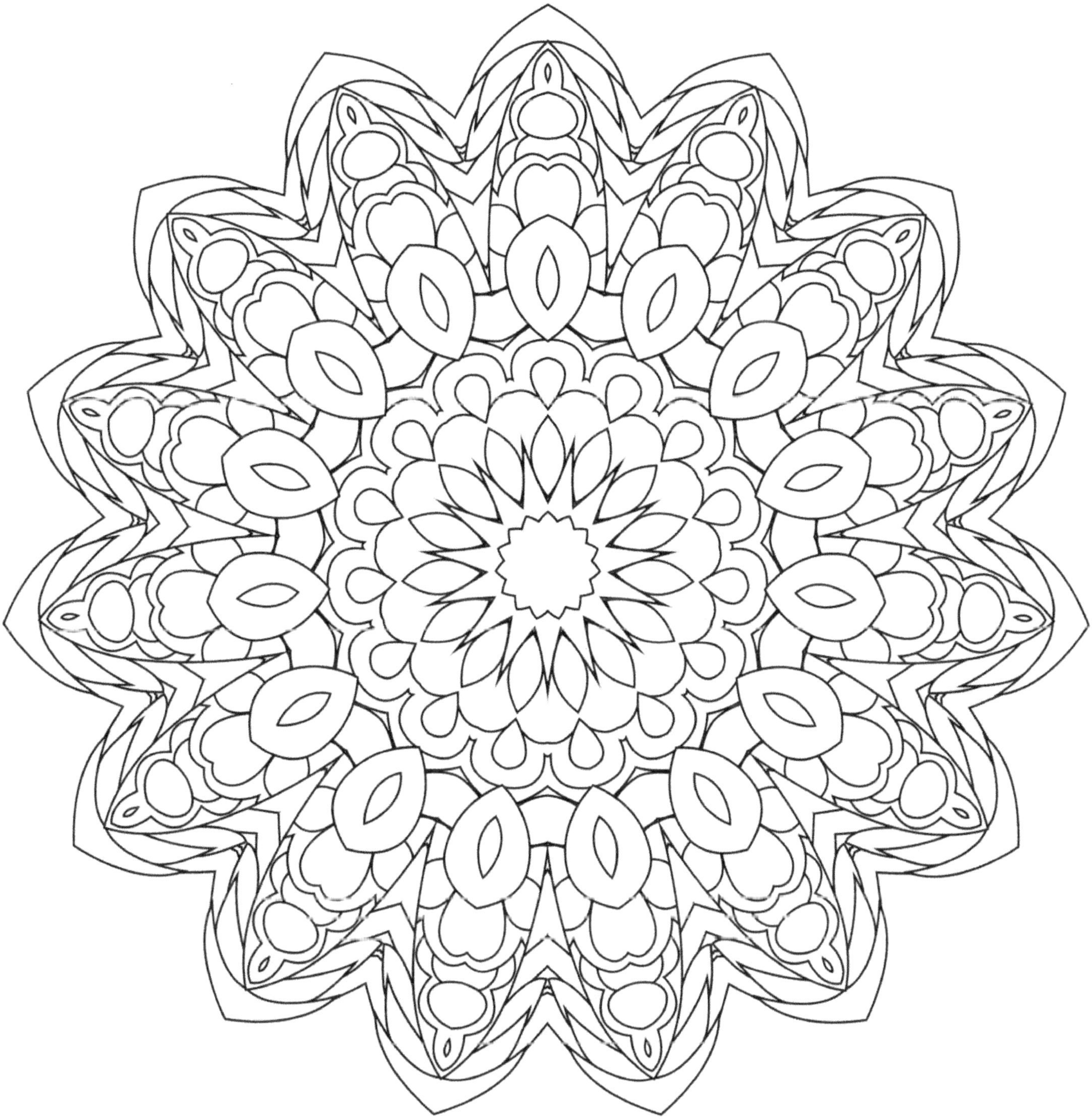

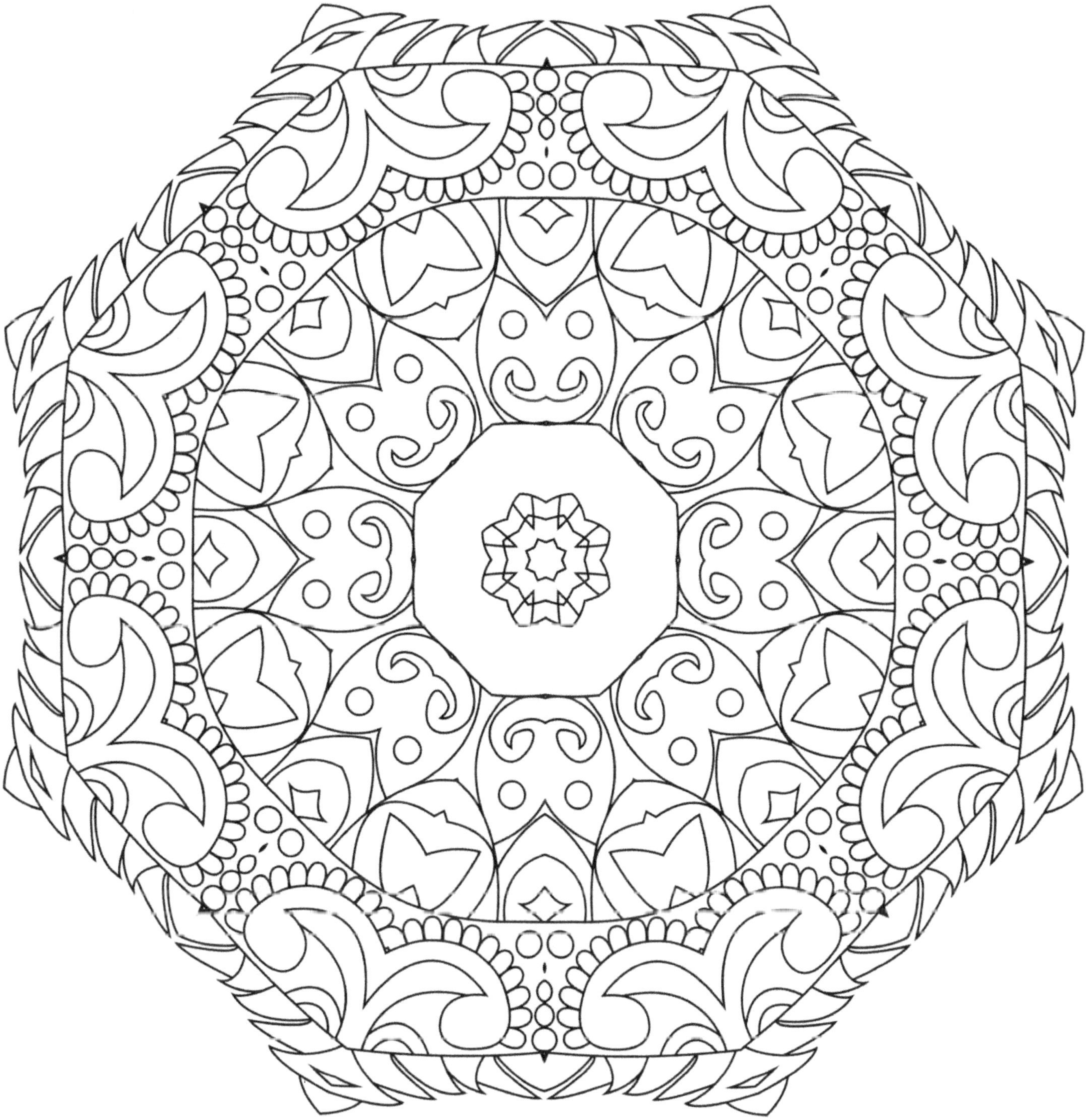

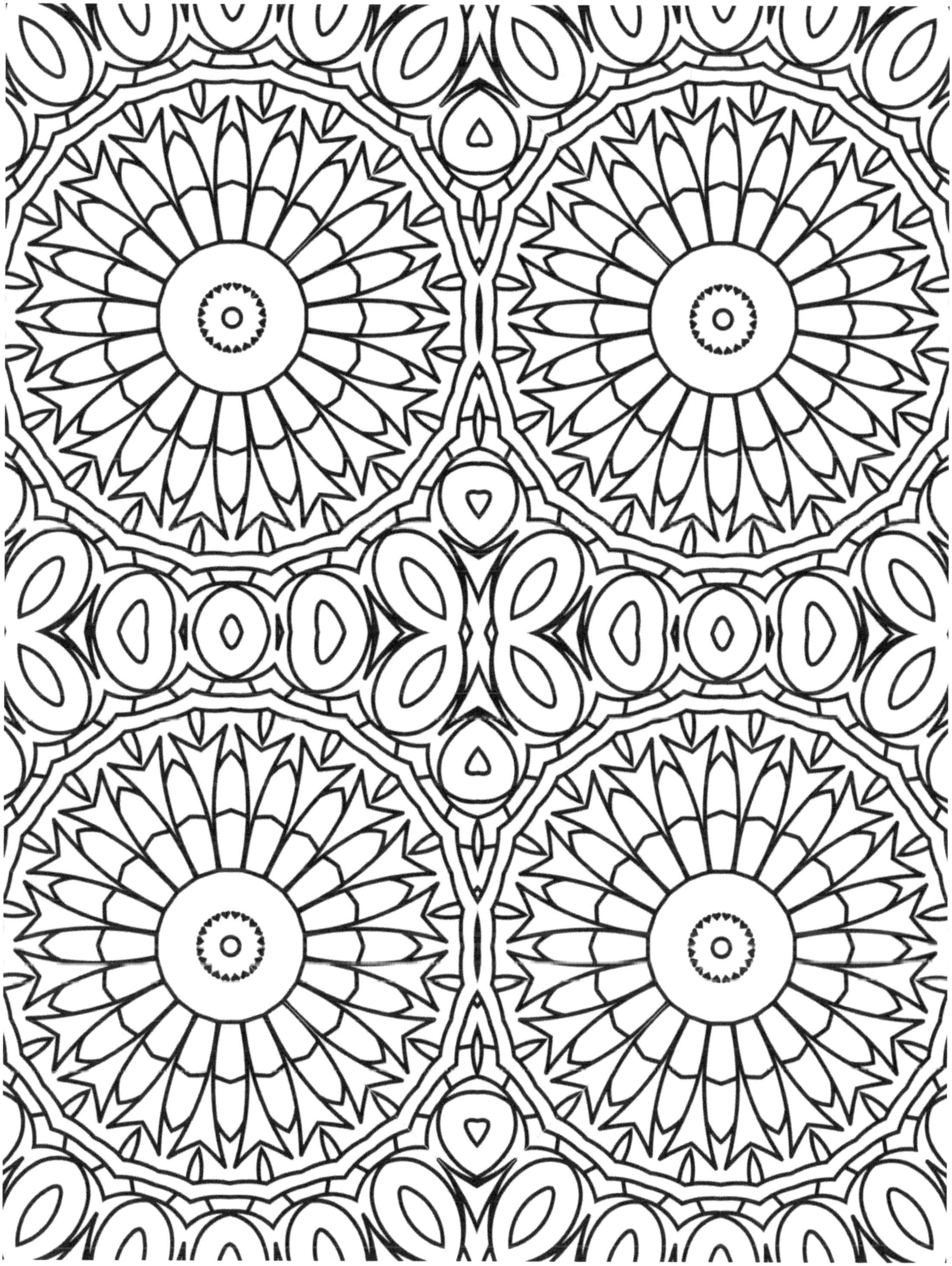

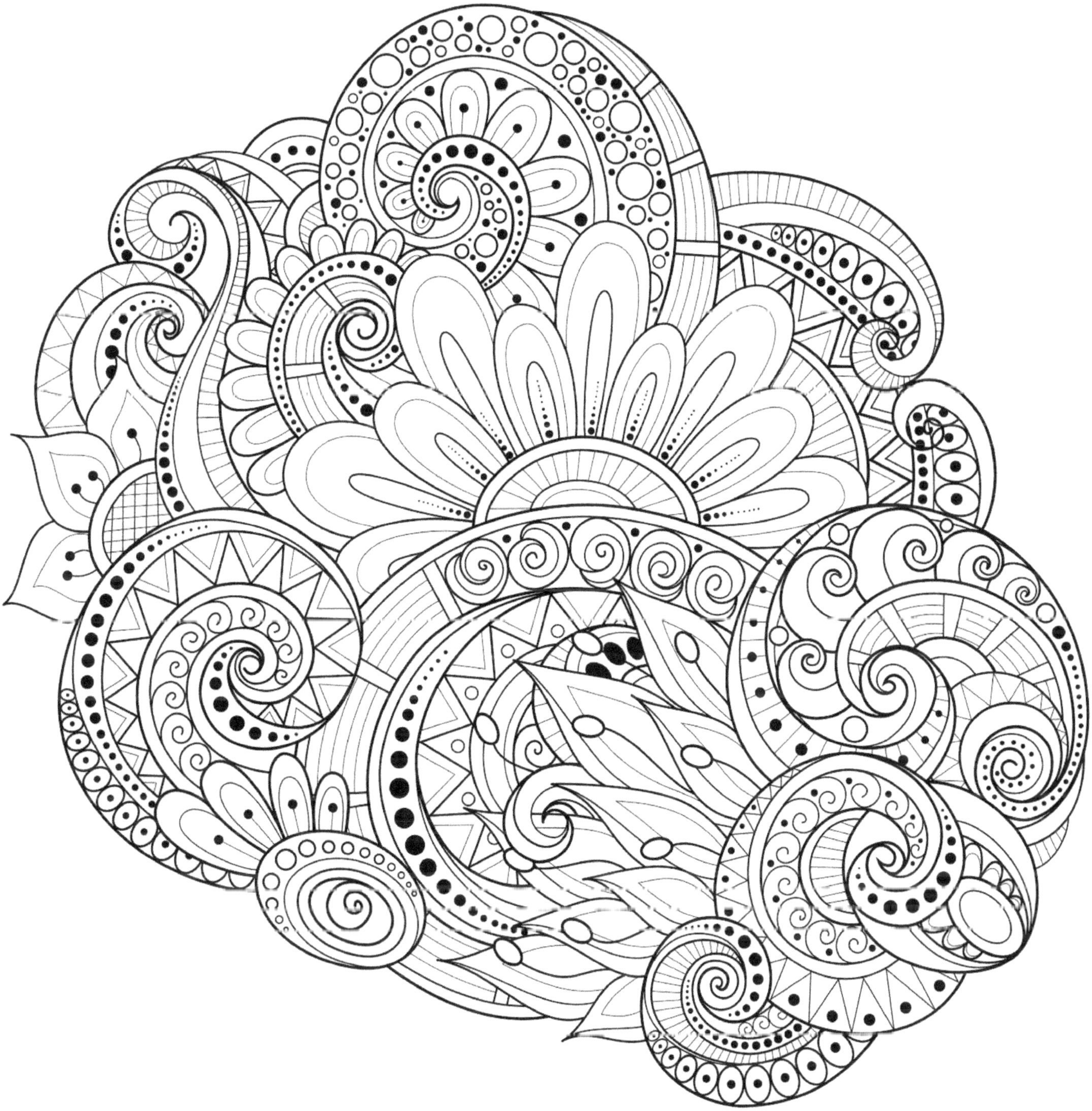

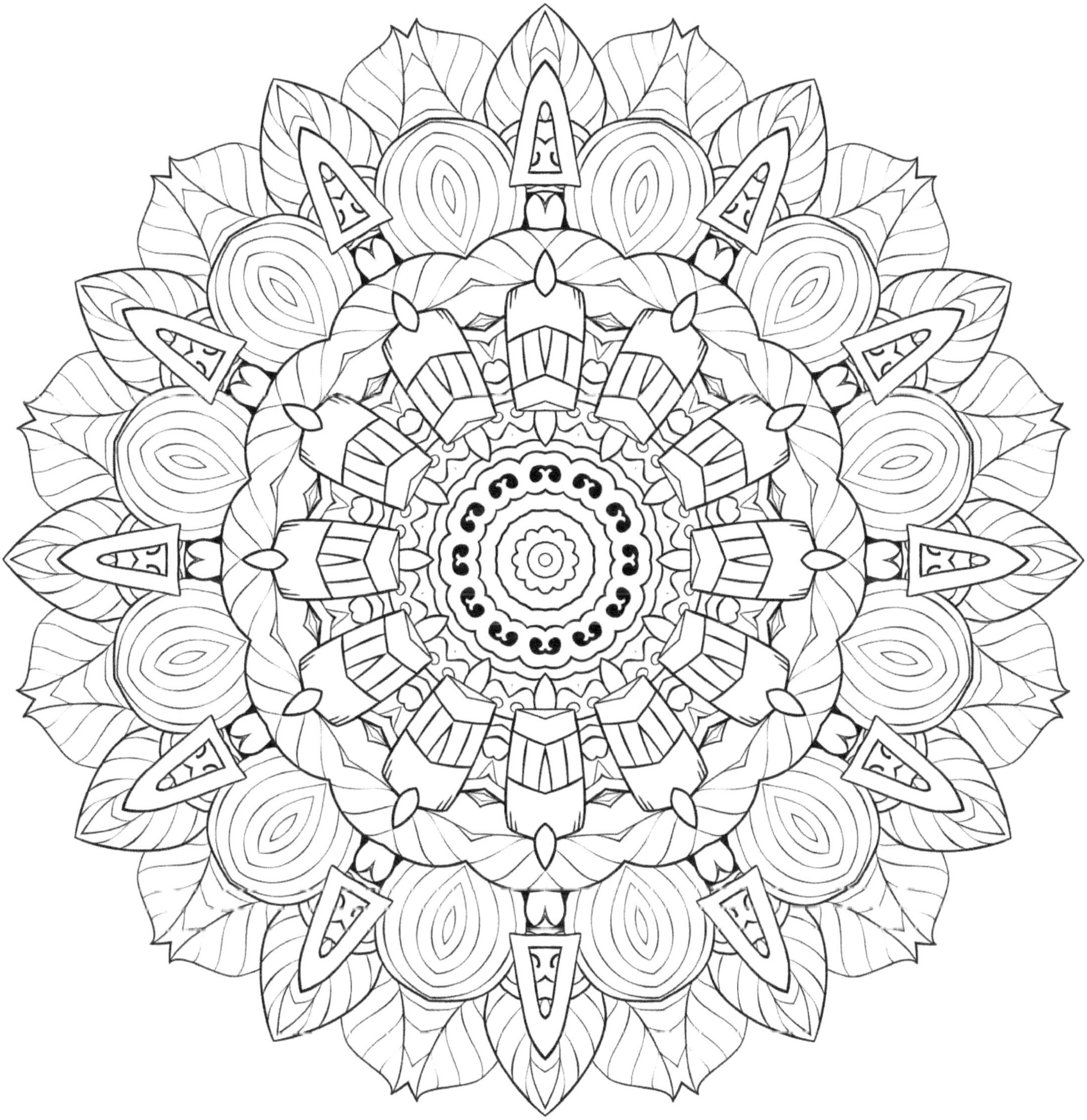

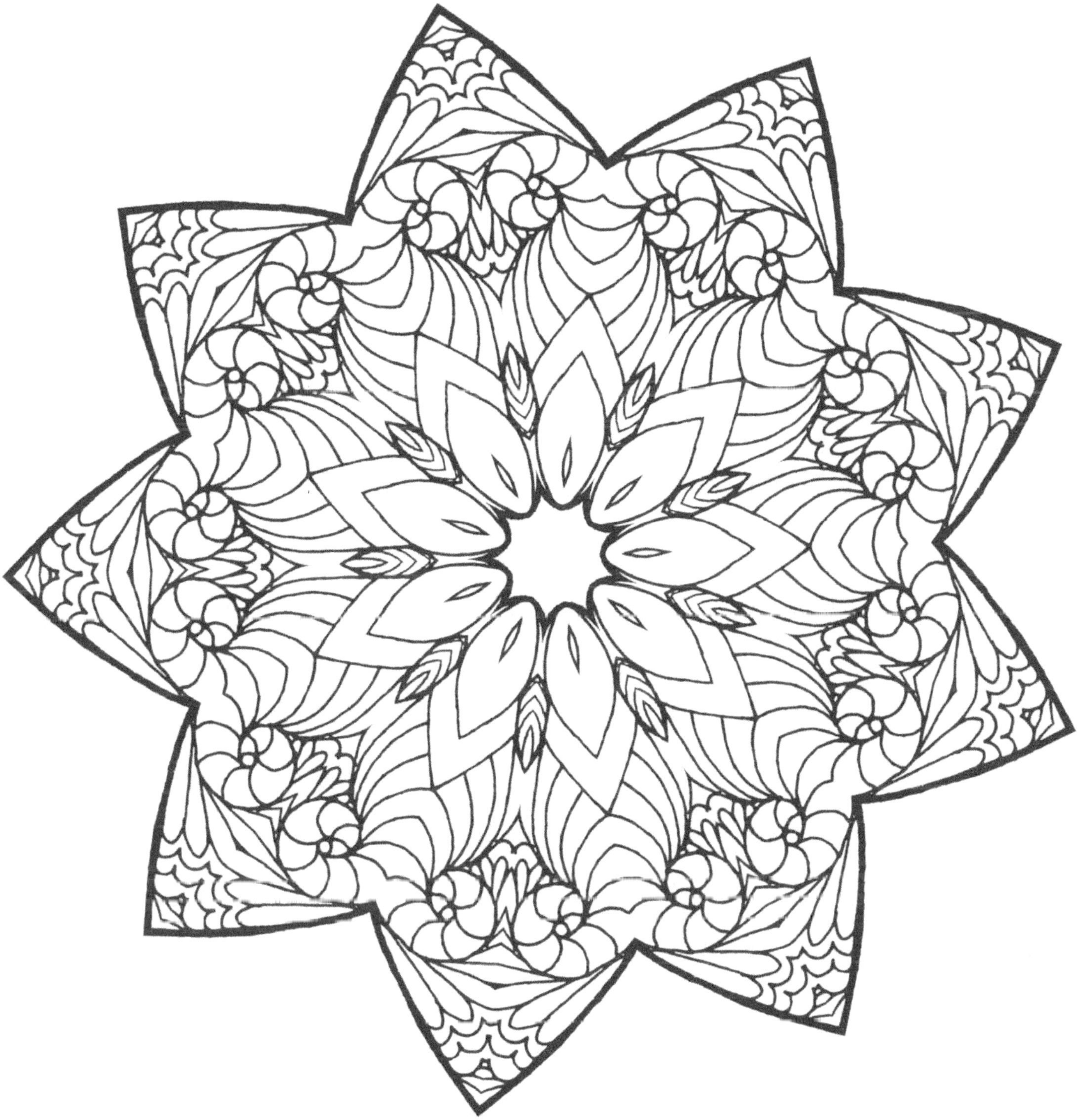

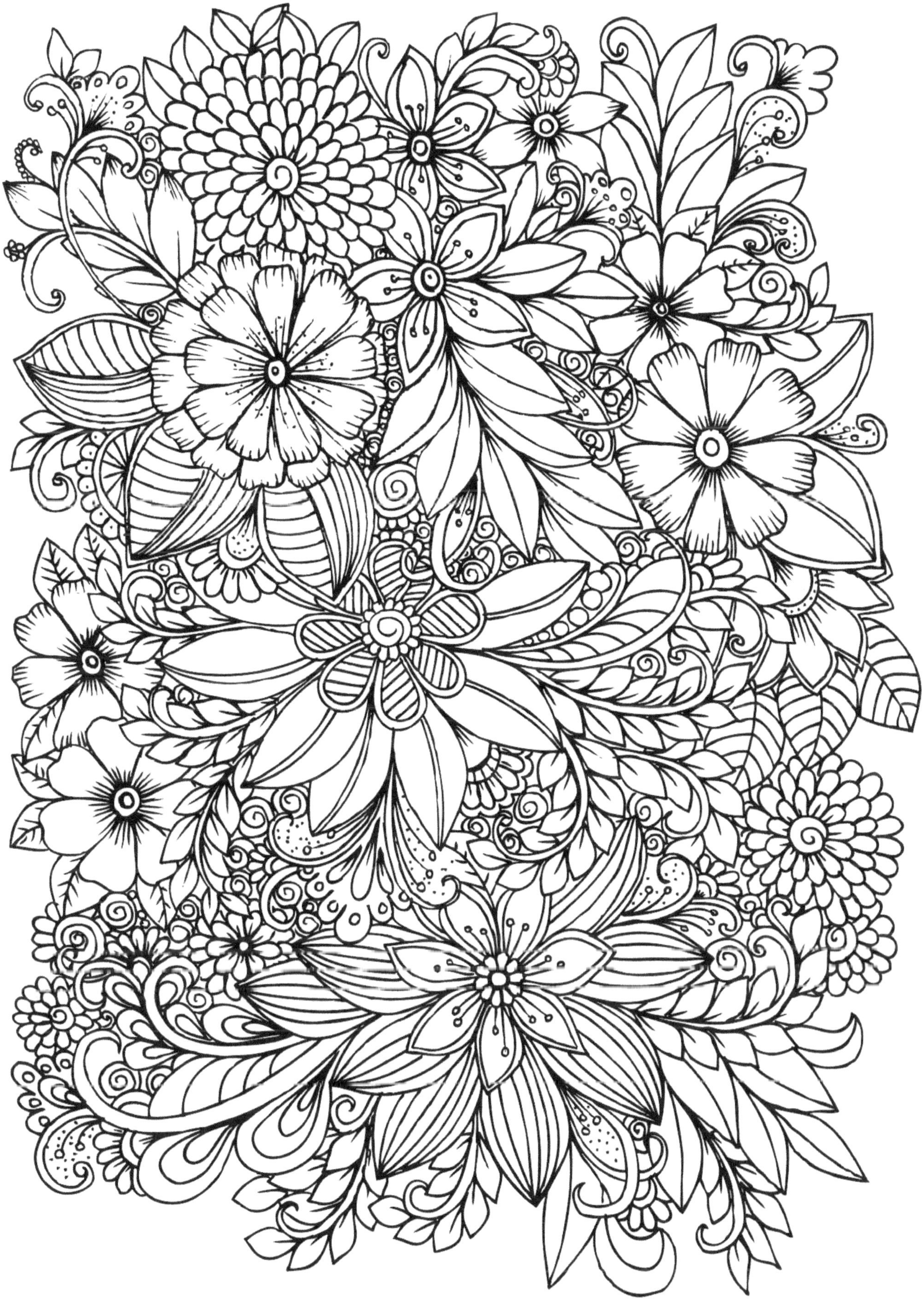

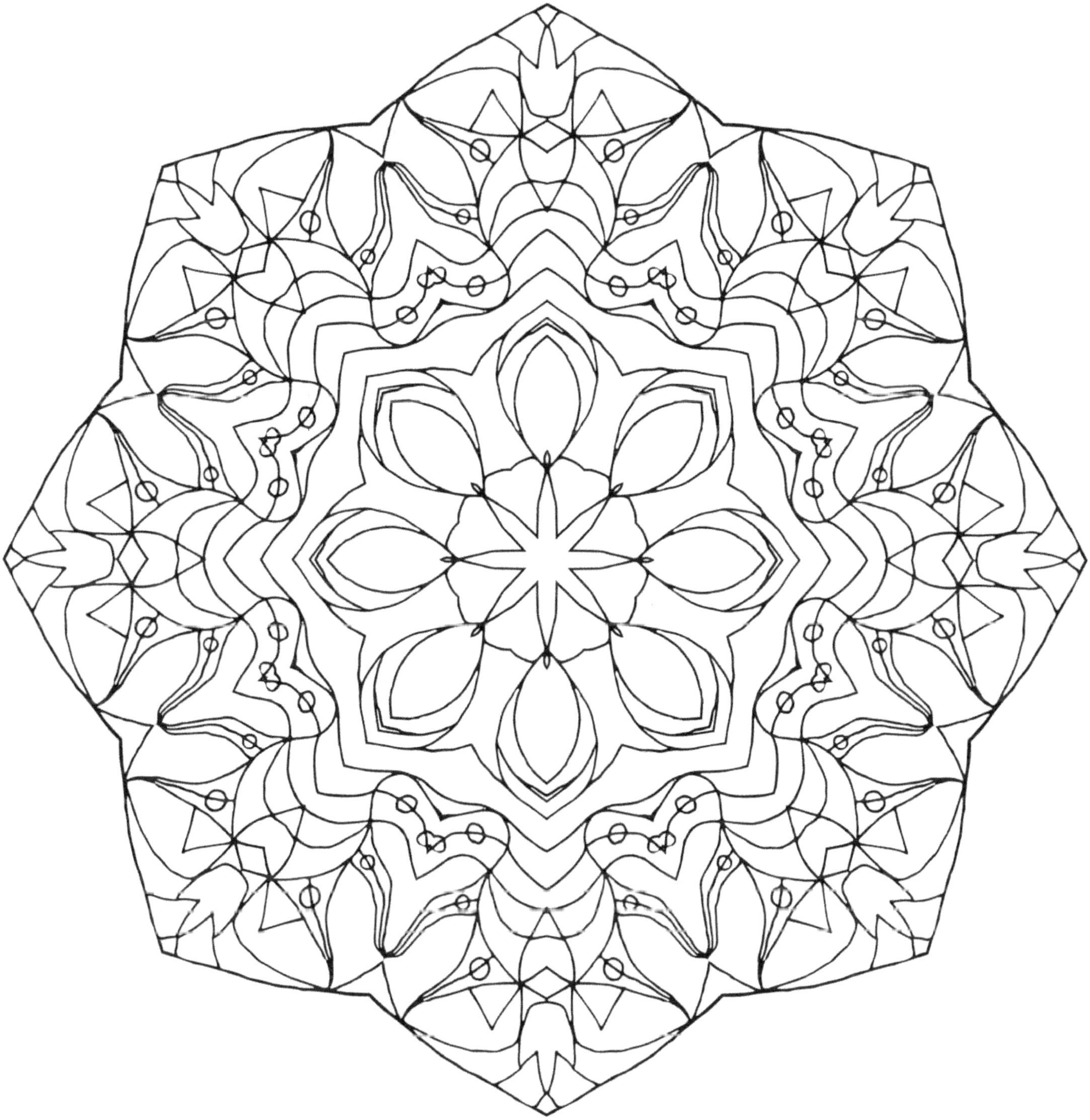

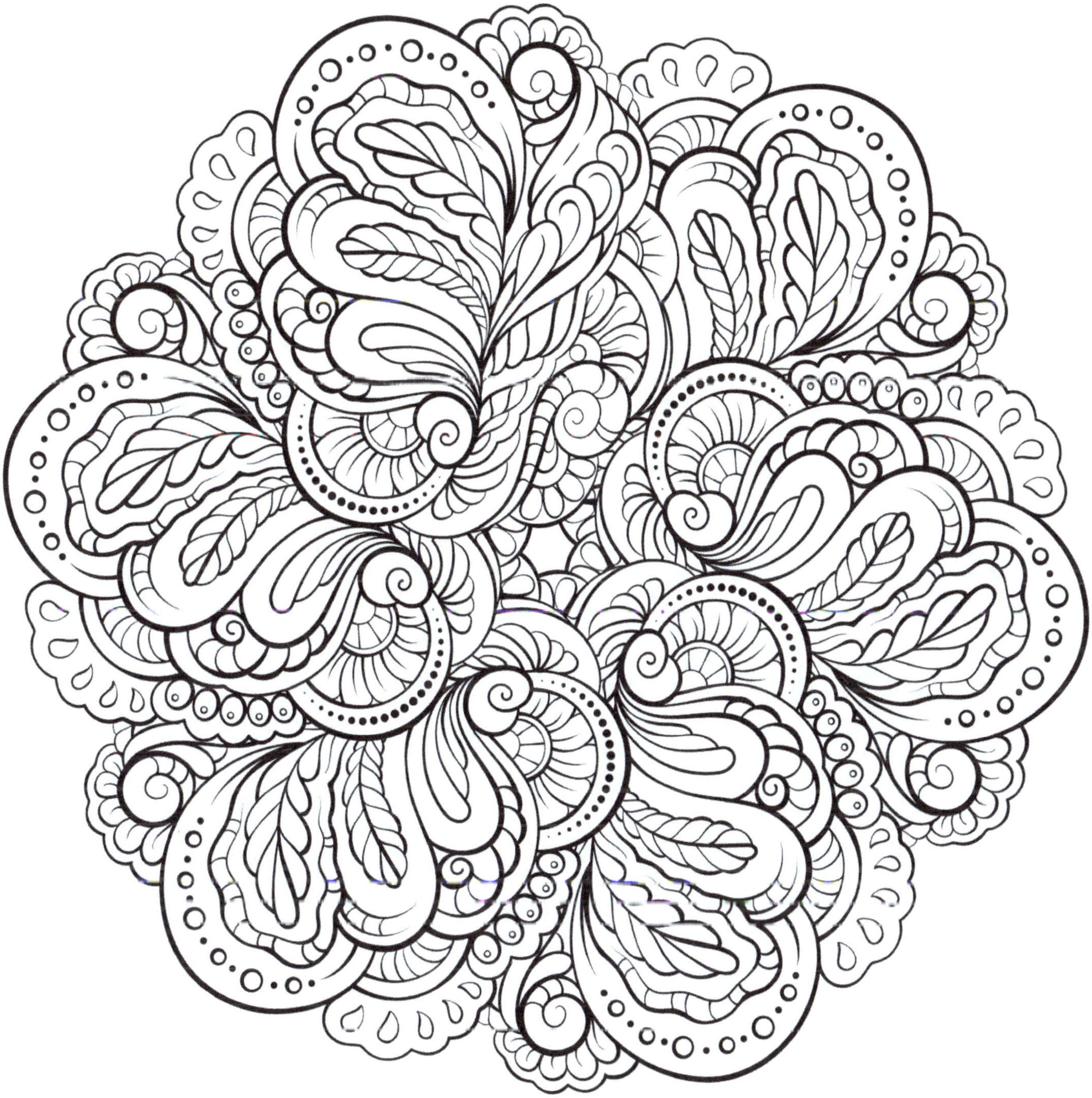

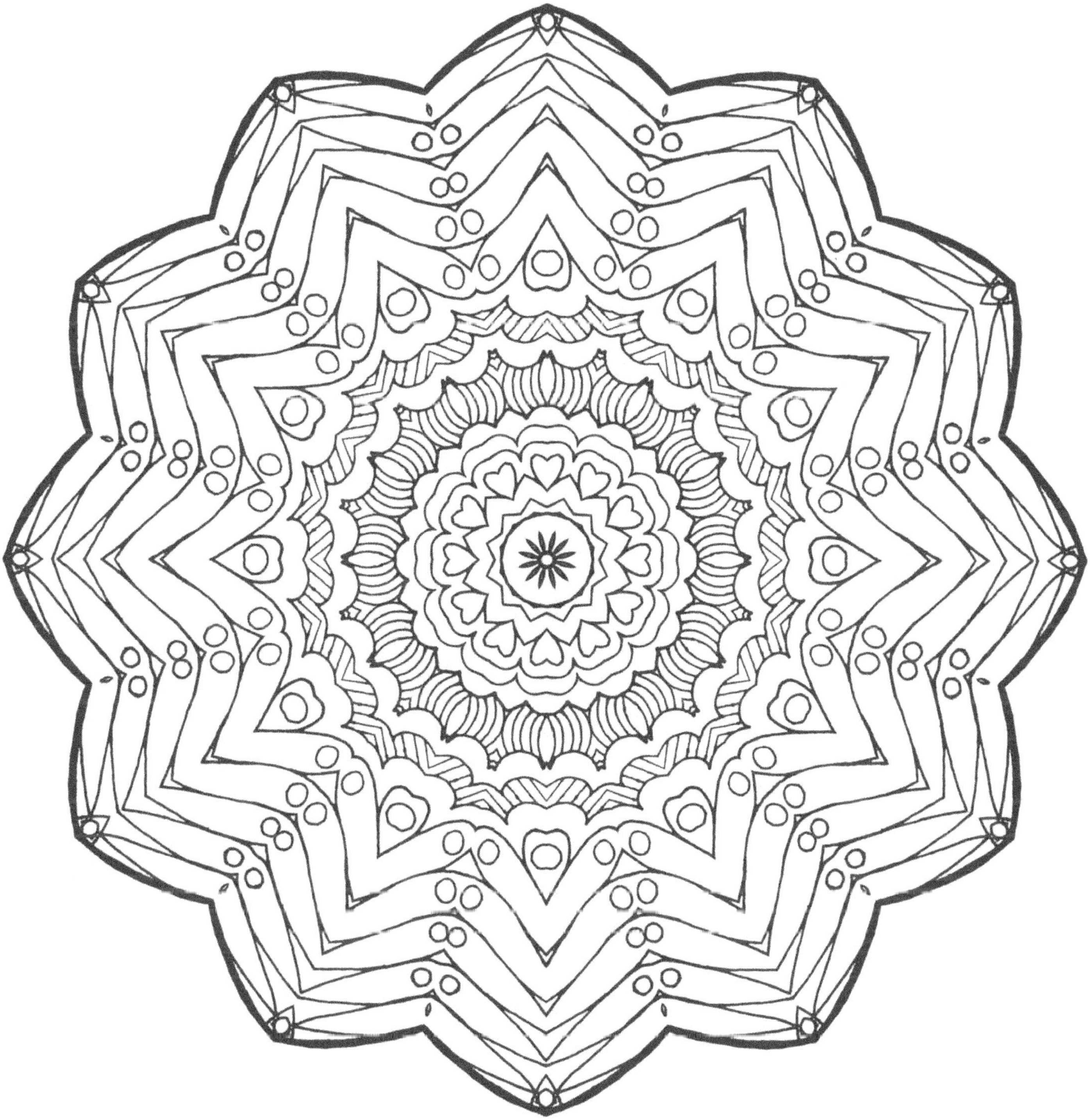

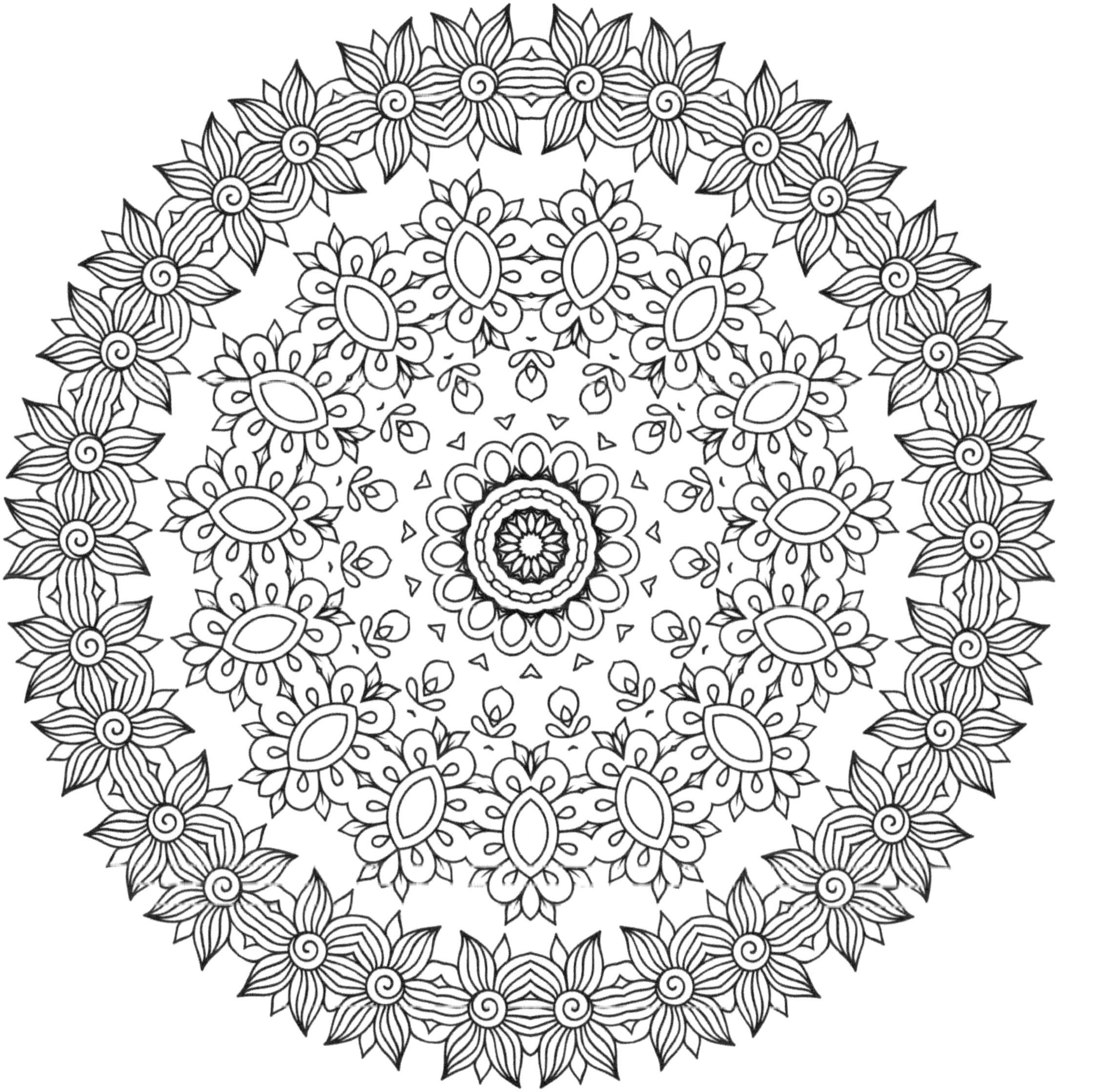

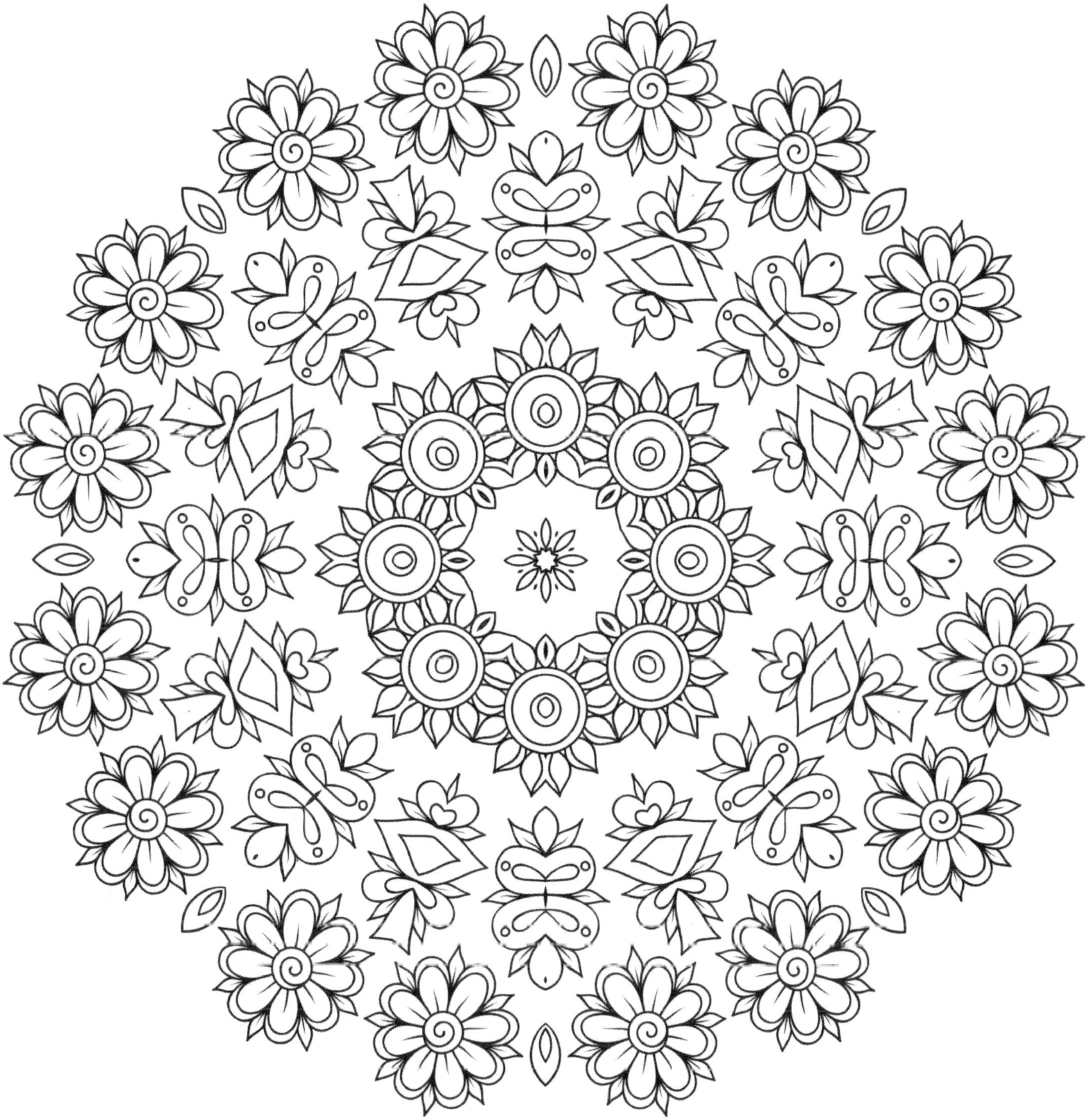

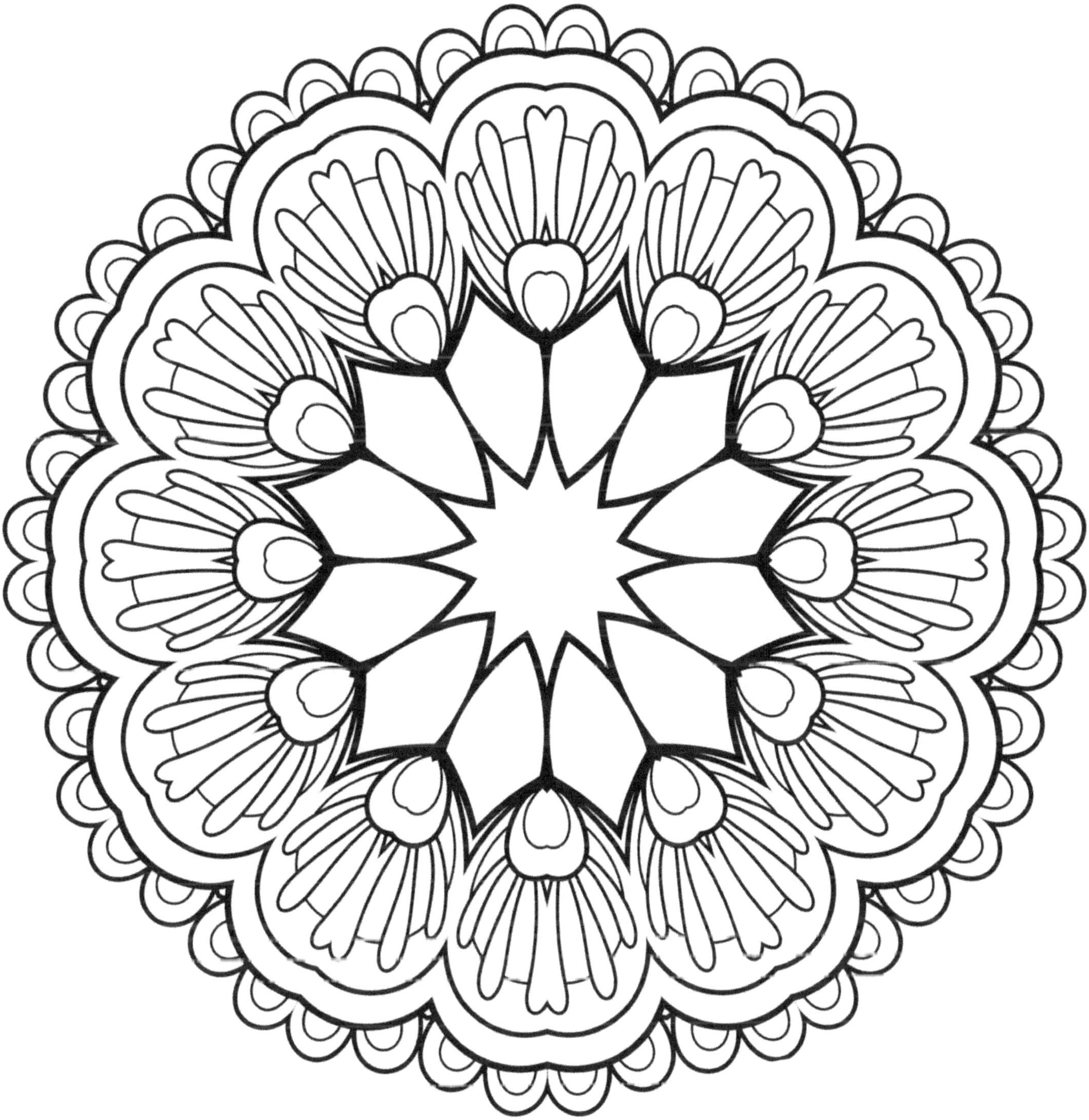

www.ingramcontent.com/pod-product-compliance
Lightning Source LLC
Chambersburg PA
CBHW081305170526
45165CB00011B/3423